Hey kids!

CREATOR Darla Hall

My name is Darla Hall and I am the creator of this activity book.
I hope you enjoy the wide variety of activities included in it.

The idea for this book began as a gift to cheer up a little boy in the hospital. I continue donating activity books like this to children in hospitals everywhere.

To learn more about these books or to purchase other team books, please visit my website at www.inthesportszone.com.

CHICAGO CUBS

© 2015 Darla Hall for National Design LLC

We hope you enjoy this activity book to show your team spirit.

2 Drawing

ME

MY FAMILY

DRAW YOURSELF IN YOUR FAVORITE TEAM GEAR

MY FRIENDS

MY FAVORITE PLAYER

4 Drawing

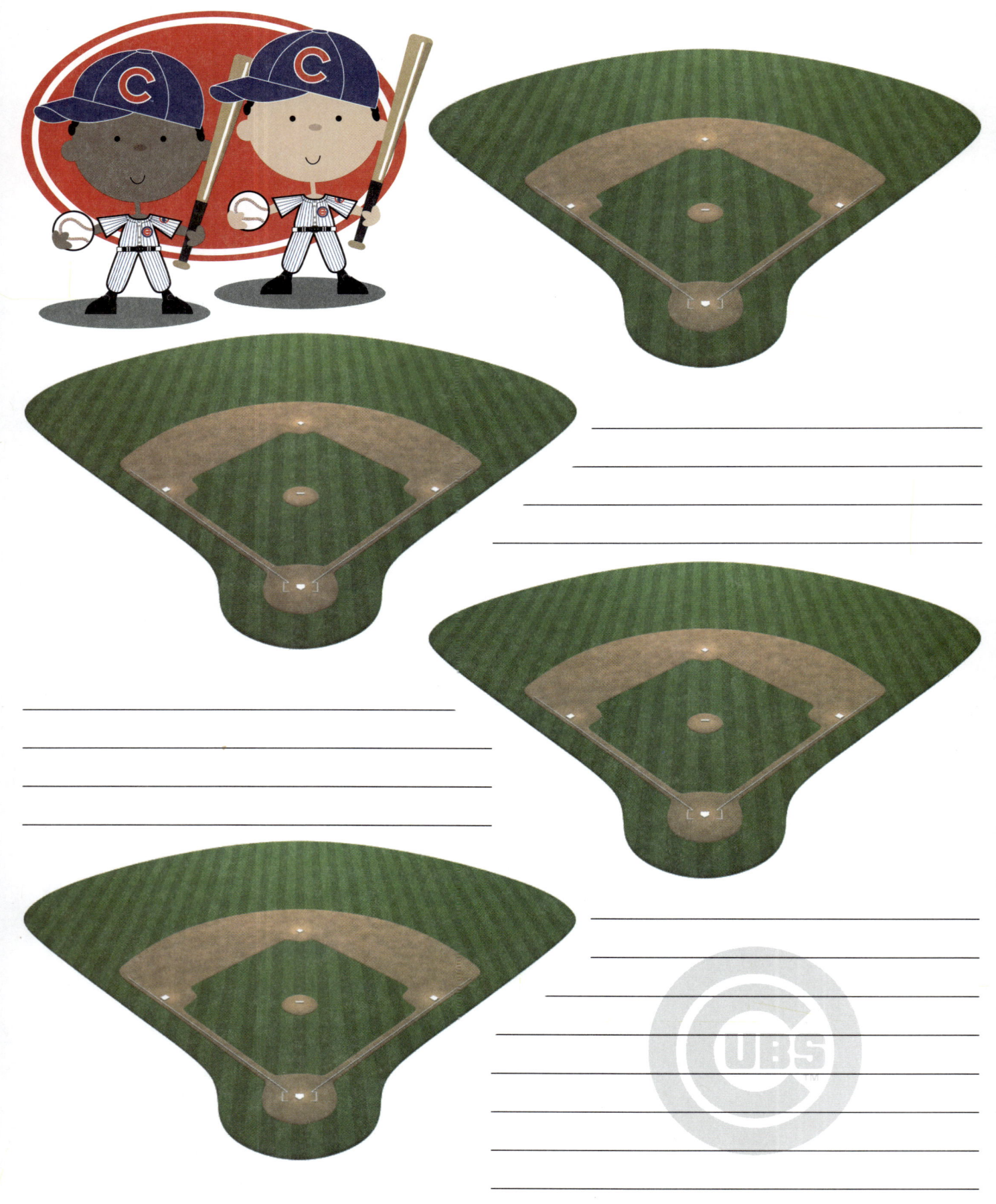

Drawing 5

6 Drawing

Draw yourself performing your favorite team song.

TIC-TAC-GO CUBS-TOE

Games 9

WORD SCRAMBLERS

1. LBBAESAL
2. BESA
3. TETBAR
4. RACHCTE
5. ITEPCHR
6. DIIEFNL
7. UOIETFLD
8. IFEDL
9. ELHMET

Mazes 11

Our Manager needs a new pitcher

help him get to the bullpen to substitute a relief pitcher!

12 Mazes

CHICAGO CUBS

HURRY! FANS ARE ANXIOUS TO GET TO THE BALLPARK!

Help them get to the game to enjoy refreshments!

GO CUBS

BASEBALL FACTS

HOW WELL DO YOU KNOW THE GAME OF BASEBALL?

Across
1. Baseball is played with a glove, ball, and this
4. This player is behind the plate waiting for the pitch
5. When the ball is hit out of the park
7. A player runs around these
8. This player stands on a mound

Down
2. Number of strikes that a player gets
3. When you get four balls
5. Batters wear this on their head for protection
6. Innings in a typical MLB game
7. Player who hits the ball

Crossword 13

14 Coloring

You are a WINNER
CREATE YOUR OWN MEDALS

Coloring 15

THE *CUBS* BASEBALL TEAM NEEDS YOUR SUPPORT.
CREATE A RALLY SIGN THAT YOU CAN HOLD UP AT THE NEXT GAME TO CHEER ON YOUR TEAM.

Game Time 17

GAME TIME!

IT'S GAME TIME! WHAT TIME DOES YOUR TEAM PLAY?

18 Scorecard

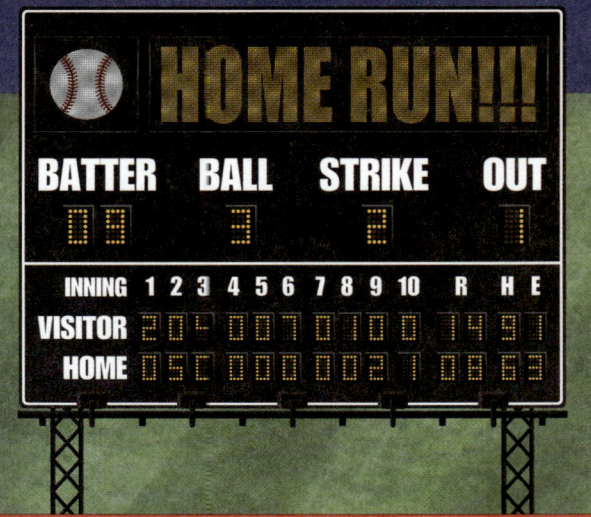

POSITION	#
PITCHER	1
CATCHER	2
FIRST BASEMAN	3
SECOND BASEMAN	4
THIRD BASEMAN	5
SHORTSTOP	6
LEFT FIELDER	7
CENTER FIELDER	8
RIGHT FIELDER	9
DESIGNATED HITTER	DH

TEAM: _____ DATE: _____ HOME: _____ VISITOR: _____

#	LINE UP	POS	1	2	3	4	5	6	7	8	9

Team Player-Autograph Cards 19

Go CUBS

20 Team Player-Autograph Cards

Here is your chance to create your own *CUBS* Team. Use these player cards to create a winning team. Or you can mix & match. There are no rules. See how your team stacks up against others. Use your imagination and make up your own stats for each player or search the Internet for their real stats.
Have fun with it!

Name
Position
Height   Weight
Hometown
History/Stats

Name
Position
Height   Weight
Hometown
History/Stats

Name
Position
Height   Weight
Hometown
History/Stats

Name
Position
Height   Weight
Hometown
History/Stats

Name
Position
Height   Weight
Hometown
History/Stats

Name
Position
Height   Weight
Hometown
History/Stats

Name
Position
Height   Weight
Hometown
History/Stats

Name
Position
Height   Weight
Hometown
History/Stats

Name
Position
Height   Weight
Hometown
History/Stats

Go CUBS

Sports Weather 21

DURING SOME OUTDOOR SPORTS, WEATHER IS A FACTOR. ANSWER THESE QUESTIONS ABOUT YOUR PERFECT GAMEDAY WEATHER.

WHAT IS THE IDEAL TEMPERATURE FOR GAMEDAY?

WHAT FACTORS MAY AFFECT THE OUTCOME OF THE GAME?

IN THE CITY OF

DRAW YOUR IDEAL GAMEDAY WEATHER FORECAST & NAME YOUR CITY.

22 Picture & Words

WRITE YOUR FAVORITE TEAM NAME HERE

HOW MANY WORDS CAN YOU MAKE USING THE LETTERS IN:

WRITE YOUR FAVORITE TEAM NAME HERE

1. _____
2. _____
3. _____
4. _____
5. _____
6. _____
7. _____
8. _____
9. _____

24 Home Run

HOW TO PLAY

Object: To make more boxes (home runs) than your opponent. You move by connecting two dots with a line to complete a box of a single square (box), the box is yours and you have made home runs. The board ends when all the boxes have been taken. The player with the most boxes (home runs) WINS!

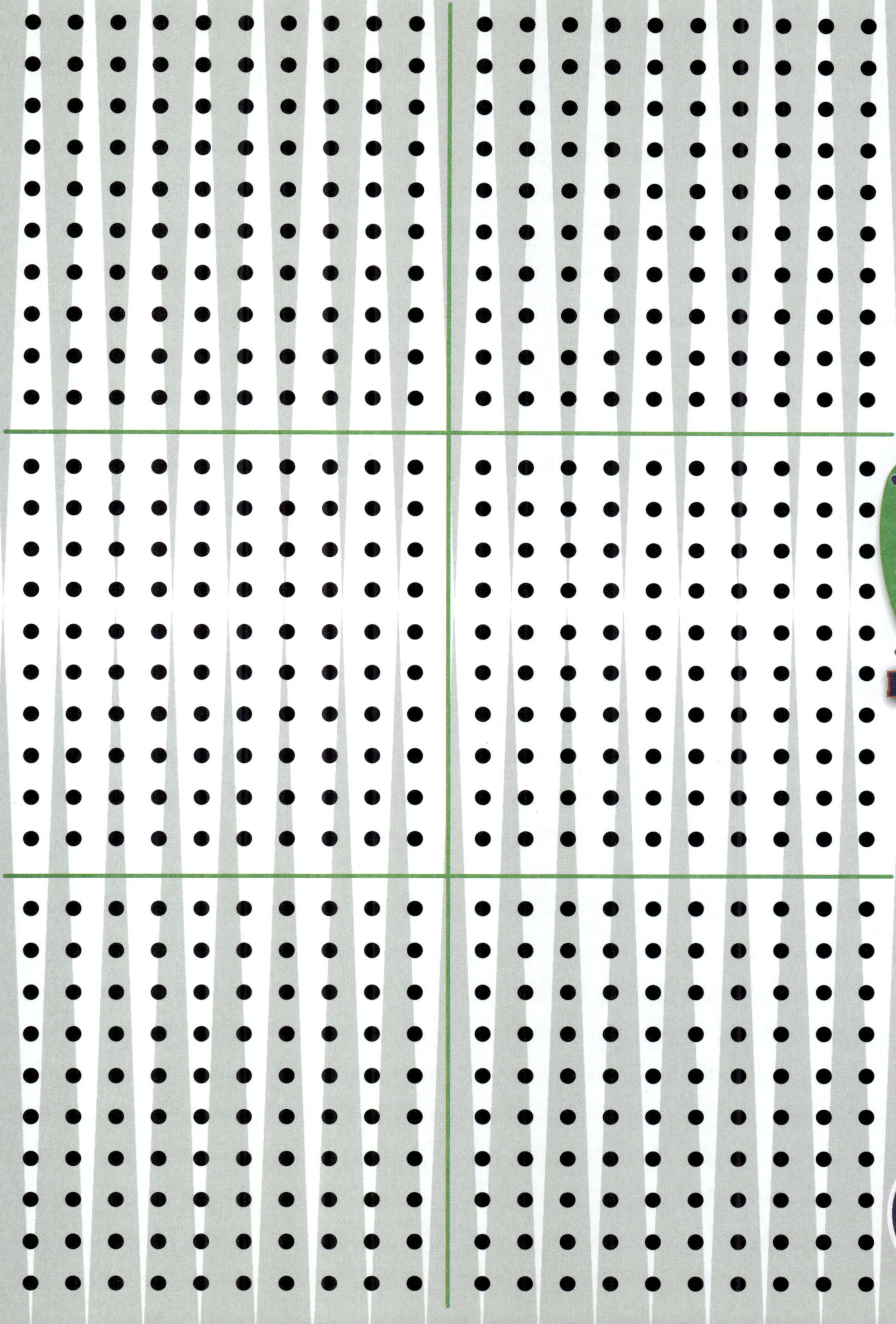

Home Run 25

26 Game Day Fun

It's time to setup your CUBS™ tailgate party!

Add your favorite foods, friends, toys, chairs, games, tables, and more! Use your imagination!

CUBS Game Schedule

Date	Game	Location	Result	W	L

28 Double Puzzle

UNSCRAMBLE EACH OF THE CLUE WORDS ON THE LEFT.

TAKE THE LETTERS THAT APPEAR IN ◯ BOXES & UNSCRAMBLE THEM FOR YOUR FINAL MESSAGE

- TRCEPIH
- RACCEHT
- FENDILI
- DIUFETOL
- SINGINN
- ABBLELSA
- TOSU
- HIST
- SURN
- COSRE
- FSNA
- MALSDNARG
- ZAGNOAITIORN

Shapes 29

DRAW A BASEBALL FIELD USING THESE SHAPES. THEN ADD PLAYERS AND BE CREATIVE. TRY TO ADD MANY SHAPES TO YOUR DRAWING AND IDENTIFY THEM.

CIRCLE

SQUARE

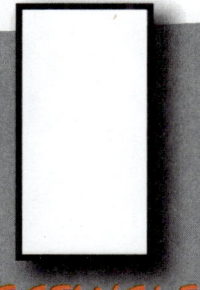
TRIANGLE

RECTANGLE

RHOMBUS

CHICAGO CUBS

30 Values

SPORTSMANSHIP

WHAT DOES THIS WORD MEAN TO YOU?

_____
_____
_____
_____
_____

LEADERSHIP

WHAT DOES THIS WORD MEAN TO YOU?

_____
_____
_____
_____
_____

FRIENDSHIP

Values 31

WHAT DOES THIS WORD MEAN TO YOU?

_____
_____
_____
_____
_____

IDENTIFY A TIME WHEN YOU WERE PROUD.

_____
_____
_____
_____
_____

IDENTIFY A TIME WHEN YOU HELPED SOMEONE.

_____
_____
_____
_____
_____

32 MLB™ Bingo

HOW TO PLAY MLB™ BINGO

PREPARE: Cut out the symbols and put the squares into a hat or bowl.

DISTRIBUTE: Use the two Bingo Cards on this page.

CALL: The caller should pull out one image, describe it and show it to the players.

MARK IMAGE: The player will then place pennies, rocks, or something similar on the called image if it is on your card.

WINNING: Once a predetermined pattern is made on a card, the player with that card calls out -

MLB™ BINGO!

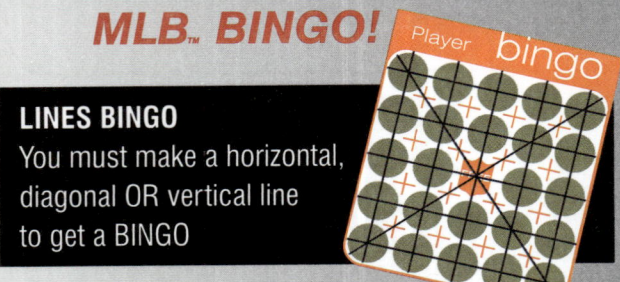

LINES BINGO
You must make a horizontal, diagonal OR vertical line to get a BINGO

Player 1 bingo

Player 2 bingo

Connect the dots

Connect the Dots 33

BASEBALL TRIVIA

Trivia 35

1. How many outs are in an inning?

2. What is a full count?

3. What does it mean to bat a thousand?

4. What is a sacrifice bunt?

5. What is an inside the park home run?

6. What is the shape of a baseball field?

7. What does HBP mean?

8. What is a single?

9. What is a ruling made by an umpire against a pitching motion that violates rules intended to prevent the pitcher from unfairly deceiving a baserunner called?

10. What is the term used when there are players on first, second, and third base?

11. What is the name of the player who squats behind the hitter and catches the ball?

12. What do players in the field wear on their hand?

36 Pix Puzzles

Can you find 5 differences in these photos?

Pix Puzzles 37

Can you find 10 differences in these photos?

38 Word Search

AVERAGE	BATS	BUNTS
DOUBLES	FLY	GROUNDED
HITS	PERCENTAGE	RUNS
SACRIFICE	SLAM	SLUGGING
STEALING	STRIKEOUTS	
WALKS	TRIPLES	

CHICAGO CUBS

Can you find these words associated with the game of baseball?

```
X B S T S I H S Z S H D U P M
D S X V T L P R N S R I E V P
E H T B A J A U D K A R T G I
D C R N B R R R V F C L N S O
N X I C U S T U O E K I R T S
U O P F Z B N B N M L A A J U
O T L F I D G T S A N V L U T
R Q E L M R A P E X E S Y O J
G U S Y Y G C T D R S K L A W
K Q Q I E O S A A O S L A M I
H K G Q R U S G S L U N N A S
R K N V M V E I N K L B K R E
S L U G G I N G N D V X L D H
N K Y B E E Z F Y B X A F E Q
H S X Q I T J O S F J U T F S
```

Word Search 39

Go CUBS

CHICAGO CUBS

BASEBALL

```
H K K G M D F S S F G D B J P
L R I K C M I Q F G R B J Y A
E F F I C I E N C Y N R O O S
D O U B L E L K N O R I U I S
S D P D M H D L W S V T N E E
T P E S T S I S S A F M C N D
U K H J T G N Q A I J N J V I
O B Z Y A E G N E G A T Q I G
T Y S M S G A L E H C J O R I
U S E Y X Z D L C R V D Y A M
P S F A A K R T I G R I F K Q
E G N A R L K N B N F O A X V
T O H V I C P Y H L G M R A Z
Z K W Q L R J Q N O Q F Y S C
U V W G T T C X D T X L V B B
```

ASSISTS	CHANCES	DOUBLE
EFFICIENCY	ERRORS	FIELDING
GAMES	INNINGS	OUTFIELD
PASSED	PLAYS	PUTOUTS
RANGE	STEALING	

40 Word Search

```
L F I N I S H E D L S A U R H
A V Q A S I B E B T O D R E M
N S R S S K R O U W W S F L W
O P B T Z E S O S D I Z S I C
I S K L A B E T H E N S V E W
T B E R O K I S U T S G X F S
N P V R I H L T T R I A U K L
E U R R M U L A O A A G I M U
T S T E G U N N U T T O S Z S
N S G G S E O W T S H O L D T
I Q I N M S A K S R T Q W D U
E N R S I L U E G A R E V A O
G V T U K N D R P I T C H E D
N A A S N G N R E I T M P A N
B W R S K S O I H Z Y Y P W D
```

AVERAGE
FINISHED
INNINGS
OUTS
RELIEF
SHUTOUTS
STRIKEOUTS
BALKS
HITS
INTENTIONAL
PITCHED
RUNS
SLUGGING
WALKS
BATSMEN
HOLD
LOSSES
PRESSURE
SAVE
STARTED
WINS

CUBS Answers 41

GAME ANSWERS

MLB TRIVIA ANSWERS
1. 6
2. 3 balls, 2 strikes
3. To reach first base on every at-bat
4. Bunting the ball, before there are two outs, to allow a runner on base to advance to another base
5. When a batter hits a home run without hitting the ball over the fence
6. Diamond
7. Hit by pitch
8. When the batter advances to first base
9. Balk
10. Bases loaded
11. Catcher
12. Baseball glove

Can you find the hidden items?
- Baseball Glove
- Baseball Bat
- Baseball Hat
- Baseball
- Cotton Candy
- Pizza Slice
- Baseball Cleat
- Hot Dog

WORD SCRAMBLERS ANSWERS
1. LBBAESAL — BASEBALL
2. BESA — BASE
3. TETBAR — BATTER
4. RACHCTE — CATCHER
5. ITEPCHR — PITCHER
6. DIIEFNL — INFIELD
7. UOIETFLD — OUTFIELD
8. IFEDI — FIELD
9. ELHMET — HELMET

DOUBLE PUZZLE
- TRCEPIH — PITCHER
- FENDILI — INFIELD
- SINGINN — INNINGS
- TOSU — OUTS
- SURN — RUNS
- RACCEHT — CATCHER
- DIUFETOL — OUTFIELD
- ABBLELSA — BASEBALL
- HIST — HITS
- COSRE — SCORE
- FSNA — FANS
- MALSDNARG — GRANDSLAM
- ZAGNOAITIORN — ORGANIZATION

CROSSWORD
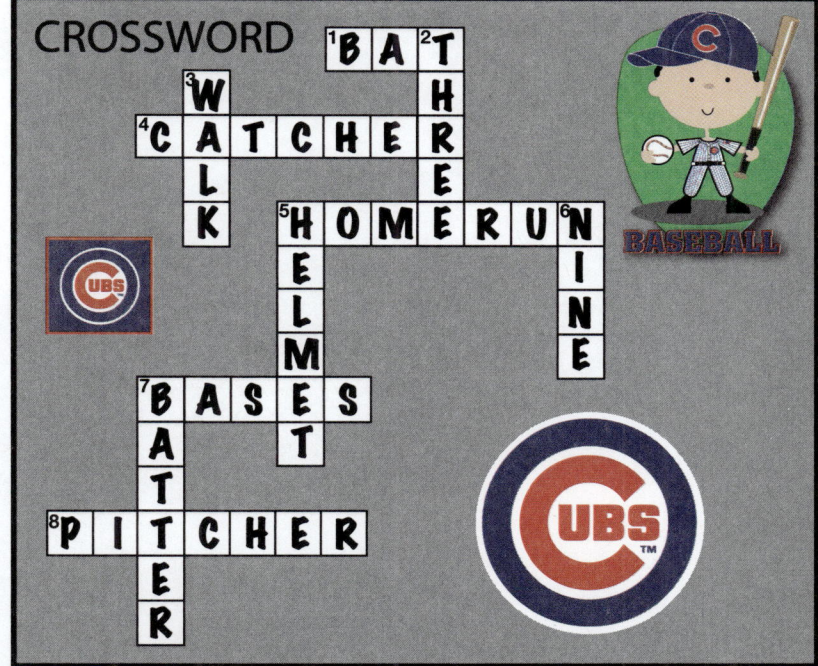

1. BAT
2. THREE
3. WALK
4. CATCHER
5. HOMERUN
6. NINE
7. BASES / BATTER
8. PITCHER
(HELMET)

WORD SEARCH

CUBS BASEBALL | **GO CUBS** | **CUBS**

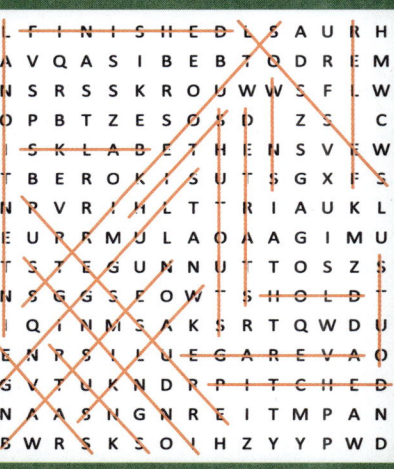

42 Writing

Here is a writing prompt for you. Your job is to finish the story. Be creative! Don't hold back. Write as much as you can. Use a lot of adjectives (ask an adult what that means if you don't know).

The Cubs manager retired, and you have been named as the new manager.

Hurry, you have a news conference in 10 minutes.

What are you going to say to address the media?

_____
_____
_____
_____
_____
_____
_____
_____
_____
_____

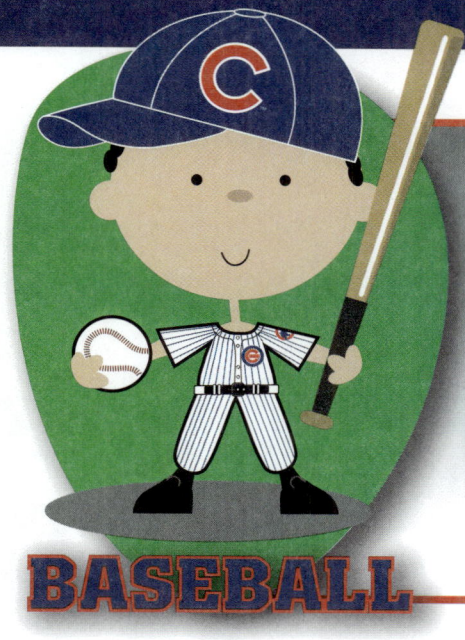

What is it that you love about *CUBS*™ Baseball?
Talk about all aspects of the game, from the managers to the players to the tailgate to the opponents, and everything in between.

CHICAGO CUBS™

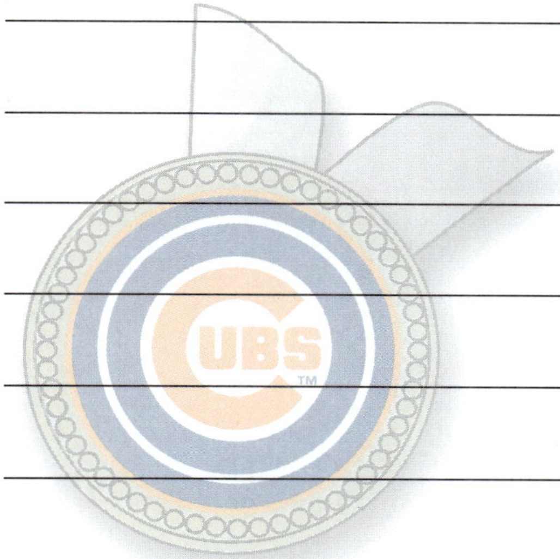

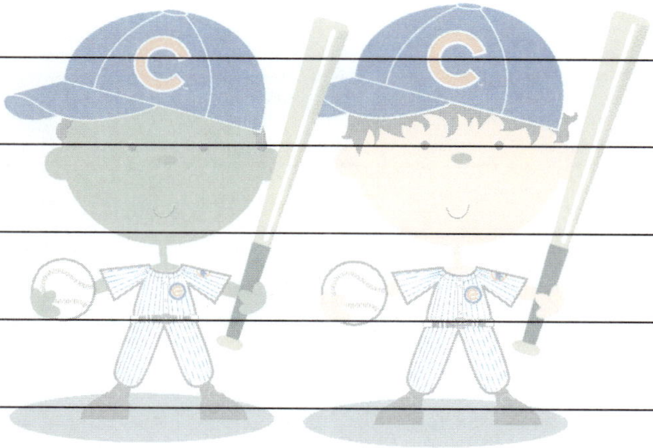

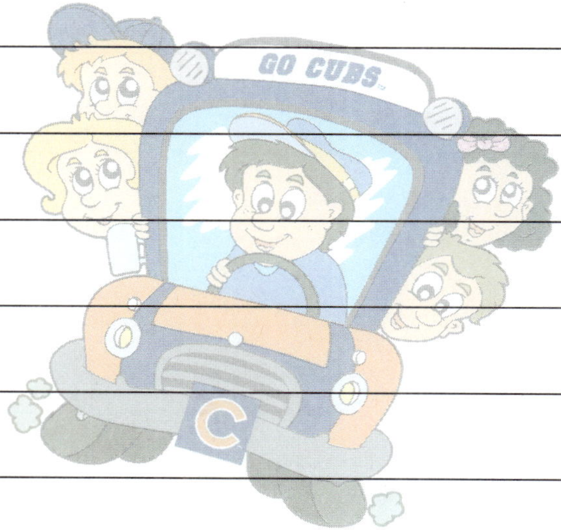

CHICAGO CUBS™

Hold on... the CUBS are coming!

You are having a dream. You are the pitcher for the *CUBS* baseball team. What would you do for your game preparation? Would you hang out and tailgate at the field? Practice? Eat? Hang out with friends?

Write a story about your day in the life of being the pitcher for the *CUBS*.

Tell us about your dream!

_____
_____
_____
_____
_____
_____
_____
_____
_____
_____
_____
_____
_____
_____
_____

Writing 45

WHAT HAPPENS IN YOUR STORY?

46 Games

TIC-TAC-GO CUBS-TOE

CHICAGO CUBS